Otherwise Unseeable

Also by Betsy Sholl

☾

Rough Cradle
Late Psalm
Coastal Bop
Don't Explain
The Red Line
Pick a Card
Rooms Overhead
Appalachian Winter
Changing Faces

Otherwise Unseeable

BETSY SHOLL

THE UNIVERSITY OF WISCONSIN PRESS

1930 Monroe Street, 3rd Floor
Madison, Wisconsin 53711-2059
uwpress.wisc.edu

3 Henrietta Street
London WC2E 8LU, England
eurospanbookstore.com

Printed in the United States of America

Library of Congress Cataloging-in-Publication Data

Sholl, Betsy, author.
[Poems. Selections]
Otherwise unseeable / Betsy Sholl.
pages cm — (Four lakes poetry series)
ISBN 978-0-299-29934-7 (pbk. : alk. paper) — ISBN 978-0-299-29933-0 (e-book)
I. Title. II. Series: Four Lakes poetry series.
PS3569.H574A6 2014
811'.54—dc23
2013033690

For David Sholl & Michael Macklin,
in memory

Flowers never die. Heaven is whole.
But ahead of us we've only somebody's word.

—OSIP MANDELSTAM

CONTENTS

III

ACKNOWLEDGMENTS

Heartfelt thanks to the editors of the following magazines where these poems first appeared, sometimes in different versions:

Arts and Letters: "Elegy with Morning Glories," "The Argument"

Bangor Daily News: "Tidal," "Russian Bells"

Beloit Poetry Journal: "Double Portrait"

Brilliant Corners: "The Aging Singer," "Bass Flute," "U.S. Clamps Down on Pianos to Cuba," "Wood Shedding," "Traps and Groove," "*Out of Nowhere*," "Rahsaan," "Bird Lives"

Cerise: "Waiting Room" (under the title "Waiting for the Shrink"), "Of the Many," "An Exchange," "Meenala, County Donegal," "Famine"

Crab Orchard Review: "Wildflowers," "The Woodcutter"

Field: "Genealogy," "Goldfinch," "Rumpelstiltskin"

Fifth Wednesday: "Atlantic City, Midmorning"

5AM: "The Clam Diggers"

Image: "Election Day" (under the title "Lord, Sky"), "Pears, Unstolen," "The Harrowing"

Janus Head: "To a Plum"

Literature and Belief: "Vanishing Act," "Prisoner Bonhoeffer"

Massachusetts Review: "What's Left of Heaven" (under the title "Blue Village")

Numero Cinq: "*Latcho Drom*," "Rush Hour," "The Wind and the Clock"

Off the Coast: "Frog to Princess"

Ploughshares: "Shrines"

Post Road: "Still life with Light Bulb," "*Poco a Poco*"

Rhubarb: "Belmullet," "Alms"

Solstice Magazine: "Sacred Heart," "At the Window"

Sojourners: "Second Line"

Sou'wester Review: "Cedar Waxwings"

"Pears, Unstolen" appeared in *The Best Spiritual Writing of 2012.*

"Genealogy" has been reprinted in *The Practice of Creative Writing: A Guide for Students,* 2nd edition, by Heather Sellers.

Heartfelt thanks as well to the folks who read and encouraged this manuscript: Susan Aizenberg, Ted Deppe, Lee Hope, David Jauss, Leslie Ullman, Estha Weiner, Tony Whedon, and to my fellows in the Portland poetry group. A special thanks to Ron Wallace. And always, to Doug Sholl, my heart.

I

Genealogy

One of her parents was a flame, the other a rope.
One was a tire, the other a dial tone.

In the night she'd wake to a hum and the faint
smell of burnt rubber.

One of her parents was a flag, the other a shoe.

The ideogram tattooed on her lower back
is the one for dog-trying-to-run-on-ice.

One of her parents was a star already gone out,
the other a cup she carried into the night,
convinced it was fragile.

One of her parents she drank, the other she dreamed.

In the revolving door of her becoming,
one pushed from inside, one from without.
Thus, her troubled birth, her endless stammer.

One was an eyebrow, the other a wink.
How they amused each other.

One was a candle, the other a bird. She was ashamed
of not burning, embarrassed she couldn't fly.

She was a girl calling across the ice
to a dog she didn't have.

Poco a Poco

Yellow practice books with their stammer names,
Buxtehude, Beethoven. And clumped notes,
dense thickets, weeds stuck to a fence,

fingers or vines—burr-tangle of stop-start,
try harder, hack through, and always
at the same place: blocked,

as if somebody at a gate or just the gate
said, "No. Not you." Some stupid password:
boy, blanket, battery, Bach. Stupid keys

stupid fingers bang till the strings tremble,
then toss the book. But the notes don't shake loose.
Notes or birds, flashing past, out of reach,

calling, "So long, sucker." Sucker
with stuck mouth, stuck piano. Or girl
making a splintery ruin. So much racket

there's a stillness after. A bird calls.
Not pretty, but it gets an answer.
So, there's try again—like tiptoe then,

finger by key, ear bent close, careful
not to disturb, like words whisper-sung,
slow, one at a time before a phrase comes,

notes before music, one hand before two,
till—*poco a poco*—finger peck
at seeds, first a few, then a flock

as outside sparrows back and forth
yard to yard don't hesitate a second
flying through holes in the neighbor's fence.

Rumpelstiltskin

From the earth I came, rain rumpled,
lichen skinned. On earth I grew old,
moss mouthed, and crooked limbed,
stubbled like scabbed trees.

But I could weave, I could turn *stray*
into *found*, feed straw to a wheel
and spin out money. I could sing,
I could goat-foot it through leaf muck

on tumbled rocks, as wind blew fire sparks
under the moon and its little moo clouds.
But not once, not once have I nibbled
and sniffed, snuggled or hummed to sleep

the tender flesh of a child,
a sweet-smelling squall, dimpled dumpling,
milk-breath spittle-grin that looks up
and loves me, me, me.

When I'd see them in baskets, in buggies
and lean down for a finger chuck,
their mothers snatched them up,
hefted them like sugar sacks.

Then I found the girl in trouble and made the deal.
She was all air, wind, blown silk, spider wisps,
and loose, runny tears—no earth to her name,
and only earth could guess mine.

Soon I was dancing around the fire,
thinking I'll have my pumpkin, my poodle,
my smooch, my clock wound backward,
my pillow to drool on.

But she grew fierce as she got round,
she sank roots, sent out little shoots that grab.
The child churned inside. The girl gripped down,
grunted him out, and then my name.

Oh, I gave the fig, I frigged and fumed.
Earth wouldn't let me mother? I stomped
till it cracked. Me, a stump post pounded down,
till I couldn't get out.

Root rot, stubble chop, rancid slime—
down I went where mountains melt
and sputter their furious sap. I wanted
something to be mine, to sing back what I taught.

Now I'm in earth's dark gut, garbled.
Nothing but me split in two. Me and want,
pressed down, cold smolder. And still more want.
Want the match strike. Want the roar.

Still Life with Light Bulb

How much energy spent on envy!
Burning all night, the light bulb knows

that an apple's still richer in the world's eye.
Though the bulb glows through fog

the way an apple doesn't—still, it's not
loved, not found at the world's start,

doesn't have its own alphabet page,
its own story of fall and attraction.

Can you read in the evening under an apple,
or turn it down low when your lover arrives?

An apple can't incubate eggs.
So, why are only apples polished on a shirt

and given to the teacher,
as if their dull inner stars could ever shine?

At least, the light bulb tells itself, nobody
draws an apple over the superhero's head

to show he's had a brilliant thought.
No, in fact, an apple's one idea

was very bad—just *eat, eat, eat me*.
And how dark the world became then.

The Wind and the Clock

The wind dresses itself in trees, handbills,
dust balls, feathers and rags—anything to be seen—
unlike the upright clock in its polished box
sure of the world's respect for synchronized
numbers, the world's need for balance and weight.

Oh wait, the wind cries, shaking the window
in its sash, aching to get near the clock,
to knock at its door, unlatch the wooden world
inside. And once there? The clock knows
the wind would toss its weights like halyards

clanging in a stormy boatyard, hurl sand
in its fine-toothed gears, or lick its many
moon faces blank. The clock has seen how
wind strews autumn leaves like clothes tossed
on a lover's floor. Ah love, the wind sighs,

doesn't love always undo the very thing
done up to draw it in? But the clock thinks,
Faceless, what would I be, my hands spun
to a dizzy blur, my numbers scattered?
Numbers! the wind cries, does love keep

accounts? Doesn't Saint Peter say a day
and a thousand years are one and the same?
To want what you can't have is a fool's dream,
the clock tells the wind. To not take what
you want—*that* is love. And the wind,

which just now was stretching its invisible flag
in long rippling waves, falls limp.
So, its argument won, the clock strikes,
as if it had no second thoughts, never
once wished for wind's little ruckus

to swirl up old hair, dried wings, dust
from the stars, dust from the dead. The dead,
for whom all ticking has ceased, who come
to mind, and then go, invisible as the—
Oh, the wind, stirring its little eddies . . .

Frog to Princess

Yes, I'm a croak cloaked in green slime,
a bulging gullet, a mouth full of mud.
But with great quads, Princess, and a tongue
quicker than flies. If you kiss me you'll taste
where life comes from, its quagmire scum,
its gnat-hazed bog of blistering muck.
Not your marble halls and canopied bed—
no, your world paves over what it needs most.

Without me where would your kingdom be?
I'm the well's pulse, its low hum of going on,
gargle of moon in its green algae gown,
bass line over which the stars flicker and hiss
their little embers down. I'm the creek's gut,
its bloat, the night's deep throat and mothering
croon. My legs gauge whether the world's going
on or out. Without me and my kind, Princess,

no pond baubles bubbling up new life.
The swamp goes silent, mud cracked, stump dry.
What are warts and a little sewer breath
to that? You pinch your face as if wishing
me trousered and pale, my voice a tenor's
perfect pitch, as if you could kiss me into
a prince with banks to bail, armies to fund.
But what you envision imprisoned inside me—

do you think a few kisses will make him
forget the mire he came from, not hear
night's mud belch and slip out to swill, slum
among moon slime and marsh rot? Princess,
when I say kiss me, I mean *me*, not him.
He's a curse, the world's hearse. I'm what you need,
your sweet amphibian bog king, the world's
wettest sex, green putty—right here—in your hand.

The Woodcutter

I look for the ones tired of standing,
old ones, not yet rotted, but weak leafers.
Then I cut the wedge, let the saw bite.

When the hard work's done, I can hum.
If I forget my dinner the woods has
nuts and mushrooms and roots.

I want for nothing. Sometimes I meet
a cross old granny or gent scolding
like a chittery squirrel. But greet them kindly,

and no telling what magic they can pull
out of a hacked-up stump. Many a kind word
softens a hard heart. Even the wolf

that swallowed Grandma just wanted
a little corn cake and beer. My brothers
are the clever ones. They shake their heads at me.

"Simpleton," they say. But I pay them
no mind. Money's what they know.
I know wood. And don't both burn?

Once I saw a lightning-struck oak
sheared off like a pencil snapped in two.
I stepped inside that old hollow heart

and breathed in its woody rot
till I thought I was afloat, or had put on
my own death coat.

I could have stayed snug inside
that singed wood, parts of it like pulpy batter
feeding all kind of crawly bugs—

not my brothers' bright buttery coffins,
but that old tree, pecker holed, lightning sawed,
a swirl of fluttery stars overhead.

Wildflowers

Consider the way they shudder in the aftermath
of coal trucks, farm trucks, the fast red car,

the way they sway in the backwind
of passing's vacuum, bending into the void,

the small rustle of what's left in the wake,
whatever is said on the edge of our leaving—

chicory, ironweed, aster, thistle, Joe-pye,
poorest of the poor—the way they stand

as if anonymous, knowing themselves
to be the blur passersby barely see,

the way they disappear when winter storms in,
and then come crowding back in spring,

the ground loving them the way it does not
love the golf course with its sleek chemical green—

coreopsis, milkweed, bittersweet, goldenrod,
sumac, wild carrot—

the way they bow to the passing waves
that release their seeds, needing only a little wind

to lift them across the field, a little rain,
a small crack in the hardpan to grow,

to possess the earth, as scripture says
they will, don't worry.

Alms

Small as a fly bump, the little voice
behind me calling *Miss, Miss*, wanted
a dollar, maybe for food as she said

in that voice of mist, so plaintive
and soft it could have come from inside
my own head, a notch below whisper,
voice of pocket lint, frayed button hole,

voice of God going gnat small. I shivered
and stopped. I looked for the source,
and there it was again, *Miss*, so slight

it wobbled moth-like on air,
up from a bare trash-filled recess
beside the post office steps. Yes,
I gave the dollar. But I had seven

in my wallet, so clearly that voice
wasn't small enough, still someone
else's sorrow, easy to brush off,

till later that night, in bed, I heard it
again, smaller—*miss, miss*, little fly strafe
troubling sleep—not a name at all,
but a failure, a lack, a lost chance.

Rush Hour

We'd been sipping wine at an outdoor café
in late afternoon light, my friend and I, our words

making light of whatever they touched, two flies
on the rim of a glass, talking as if the sky admired us.

Then out of the skateboards, bass thrum and laid-on horns
of jammed traffic, a woman appeared beside us,

set down her canvas bags, and the way her fingers flew,
it was clear she was deaf, signing a kind of shriek

at the street, at the cars and the awning over us,
which I saw could any minute collapse.

Small cross at her neck, short hair flecked with gray,
smudged glasses sliding down her nose,

the woman leaned in, flicked her hands toward my face,
so I looked up, away, then back, and had to shrug,

"What? I don't understand." Staring at me,
she conked her head three times with the heel of her hand,

and who couldn't understand that?—
bang against the world's bony ears,

whack to shake something loose,
tell the Furies, "Back off, settle down."

The light changed, she gathered up her loose
handles and straps, stepped wordless into the glint

of bumpers and hoods. In her wake we watched
light drain from our glasses under the thinning sky,

watched her move through sirens, skate clatter, taxis,
snatches of rap, and what could we say

that wouldn't leave everything inside her
unsaid?

Atlantic City, Midmorning,

and a woman still dressed in last evening's
green sequined gown looks pale, spent,
in this harsher light, as if all night

she's been chasing, reaching too far, grabbing
for any stone or shell or salted glass the tide
tumbles in. Now, without lifting her eyes,

she pushes more chips onto the felt.
Outside the city's glittering windowless rooms,
waves rise to a curl, then calmly subside.

But what if the ocean got tired
of being no more than a nightclub logo,
a peeling billboard on stilts, got tired

of people gazing through glazed fixations?
What if those green fathoms gathered themselves
into one enormous swell?

It could rage through this town,
or if it wanted, just rough up one woman
already shedding sequins along a split seam.

The rubble line's all about loss, loss rolling
through waves that toss their load of shattered dice,
loss seeping up the hem of the green gown,

as if that's what she wanted all along—
loss like the turned-out silk of a pocket
when luck goes cold and there's nothing left

but noon light gleaming on boardwalk slats,
glinting across the simmer of waves, light
erasing all but its own brilliant self.

Tidal

Blue inlets, blue ebb and flow, blue ether,
other, over, blue ovens of air, orphans
of wind drifting in night skies, blue Monday,

and Tuesday's just as bad, music played
on the piano's stained teeth, some so black
they're blue—Sister, who were we

that we were told never to groan or wail
or act "common"? How did you know
to give the piano all those forbidden sounds,

your fingers on the keys, climbing scales
day after day? Repeat, repeat, blue Bach,
blue Beethoven, Ravel unraveling,

and the shoreline in endless flux, nothing
finished that's not undone, blue-black mussels
sprung open. Blue yarn, blue notes, ink,

houses we built so well the wind has to
blow hard to loosen the roof, make us
unlatch our wounds, and love our ruins.

The Clam Diggers

Addison, Maine

Through grit thicker than coffee grounds,
they bend to look for what bores in

and spits air bubbles out. They dig
for what's hidden, what clasps itself shut

and keeps its secrets. Each clam's a coin
in the pocket. From the shore it seems

a poor way to keep the bank off their backs,
their backs bend double over mud beds,

looking down at darker selves staring up.
But, clearly, they know what they know,

how shallow leads to deep, how nothing keeps
back the tide's turn, stops algae from closing the flats.

When the last of the tide trickles out
they step into muck that sucks their boots.

Gulls shriek in morning fog, mud gullies drain,
then slowly fill. They know what drags a body

down, what lifts it up, what squints an eye,
stiffens a back. On this strand where the sea

seeps in and the shoreline drifts, makeshift
is how they live. On wet silt and sift they stand.

Rahsaan

The sun sets off a whole lot of vibrations . . .
Sometimes on the tenor I try to get a sun sound.
—RAHSAAN ROLAND KIRK

"You think I'm a clown?" He hits the switch
and the dressing room goes blind. Now who's
master of lights out, guide through the starless night?

Inside that vivid pitch, he hears flute-talk,
half goldfinch, half wheeze, hears a horn his dream
calls *moon zellar*, its banged-up metallic mouth.

Though sound has no weight, it needs a bell
and reed, needs muscle, breath, two puffed cheeks.
It can use a man with a bag full of horns,

willing to walk the rim between trickster
and sage, a man with the grit to keep going
if a stroke nails one hand down.

Certain sounds lie buried, heaped up, unheard,
till someone comes along with a cellar
behind his eyes, and inside that

a furnace blaze of dreams, a rush of notes
like coal shuttling into its metal house,
sound of flashlit siren-scan catching the gleam

of brash, a high C's shattered glass—
a man who says, "You want to hear sun vibes,
wind in B-flat? Well, shut your damn eyes."

Bird Lives

My neighbor's license plate reads BRD LVS
like that graffiti grieving fans first scrawled
on walls and sidewalks after Bird's last riffs,

strung out, half broke, balanced on a cliff,
blowing hard as if that could stop the fall.
My neighbor will tell the town BRD LVS,

and music has no grave, bebop still thrills.
He revives the words but with the vowels
lost like missed notes in Bird's late stumbled riffs.

Musicians crash, but leave behind their gifts:
"Camarillo," "Ko-Ko," "Parker's Mood"—all
those tunes make my neighbor right: BRD still LVS.

On vinyl, tape, CD, live patrons shift
in their seats, cough, light smokes, and one calls
Oh yeah, as Bird pours out a liquid riff.

My neighbor's not into nostalgia trips.
He knows what jazz cost Bird, head to balls,
so pays for passing cats to read BRD LVS,
to know what life was blown inside those riffs.

The Argument

September 1, 2009

On my way to the library,
sunlight on the first turning leaves,
goldenrod, coreopsis—and the crows
have something to say:

> *For the sake of the dead, for the sake*
> *of the murdered, don't wax too eloquent*
> *here under these dust-choked trees.*

Clear sky, seventy years since
Hitler invaded Poland, and we are here,
just one stray cloud for contrast.
But now a chorus of bleak thoughts,
a tree full of black fruit:

> *For the sake of the horses those Poles rode out*
> *against panzers and planes, for the sake of the spur wounds*
> *gouged in their sides, their buckling legs, for the men*
> *on their backs still human as they fell, and the other men*
> *inside their tanks turning into machines . . .*

Oh lighten up, I want to say. Morning glories
have scaled the stop sign, school buses are making
their first practice runs. The world goes on.
Still, the crows, those irascible grievers,
ratchet up their cries:

> *Goes on? Like bullhorns given over to endless*
> *yammering channels? Like this gasping hound*
> *the woman can barely contain on its leash, straining*
> *after a squirrel, a sunning cat, now you?—*

> *You, with your own black heart, carnivorous and wingless.*

Okay, okay. But can't I praise this late
summer day, the air rinsed clean?—and don't say,
Good for invasion. Let me have this brief walk
to return seven picture books showing children
a world of order and cheer, bears in ruffled aprons,
singing badgers—

and, I would like to point out, not one crow
tugging at roadkill guts, relishing the sound
of its own backfired voice.

But overhead, on a wire slung across the street,
that row of frayed umbrella wings—as if a clear sky's
no protection—and one rusty croak:

> *For the sake of the murdered, for the sake of the dead,*
> *for all that hasn't happened yet . . .*

II

What's Left of Heaven

I longed to put them down on my canvases,
to get them out of harm's way.
　　—MARC CHAGALL

Not in a museum or book, but in sleep I saw
those paintings, little man in blue pants
afloat over the town, his violin

playing the screech of crows flying up
after the first shot. Then many more rounds,
and a whole town rises—cow and bridge

and jumbled houses, wagons and goats
and red onion roofs flying apart. First
they fall down, hit hard, then rise back up

into the air, what's left of heaven. There is
a bride whose two feet don't quite touch earth,
a horse's eye—Oh Chagall, the past adrift,

cut up in wedges, the jagged glass become
blue windows into the *gone*, the *never*, the *once*,
held only by color and lead, longing and sleep.

Your tipsy villages crimson with flames,
where citizens pulled out toilets, church pews
and old sinks to stack up against panzers—

when I was young I thought that was *history*,
meaning *over and done*. Still, my dreams filled
with locked boxcars blurring the countryside

into streaks of color, the land through slats,
ghostly Bauhaus barracks with Prussian red
chimneys at the track's vanishing point,

as if sleep were insisting the *gone*
is not *over*, though the *once* will never return
to women wailing for their dead,

to men on crutches with sock-covered stumps,
and other men with eye patches over
the last thing they saw fly into their faces.

At night when the stars look like fat asters
blowing across the sky, I try not to think
of explosions, gas fires, burning trash,

of old wars whose winners carve up the world
into pieces that rub against each other
until sparks fly and flames erupt

that will scorch us all. Oh Chagall,
good to remind us of cows, hens, the moon
dangling from its rusty hinge, a fiddler

on his green violin, and the bride waiting
in midair for a man whose white shirt
blooms with dark roses. She drifts, silent,

moth-like over broken stalks, bearing no tools,
but a glass raised to the song that won't stop,
to the groom who hasn't yet come, to the world

that's still undone, its sparks and its young
who can't imagine that the light they see
comes from everything they love slowly burning.

Goldfinch

*"My goldfinch . . .
together we'll look at the world . . ."*
    —OSIP MANDELSTAM

The way you sit at the feeder, your head cocked,
beaking a seed, I think of Mandelstam
mumbling, working sounds out of their husks.

And that flash, that song made in flight,
that high-pitched muttering—

How fragile genius is,
anxious, always ready to leap from the sill,
always an eye out for the informer . . .

Wings black as tilled earth
folded like hands behind your back.

What did he think, little one, reciting
"the ten thick worms of his fingers," reciting
"scum of chicken-necked bosses"—

reckless as it was, still better
than whispering in the kitchen, hiding
behind the radio's storm?

Every spring you bring him back to my yard
as if you've memorized the address.

And you call, you call
like a phone still ringing in a house
whose occupants have disappeared . . .

Russian Bells

Soviet law made the ringing of bells illegal in 1930.

Back then monks pulled the heavy ropes, toll
after toll, so the tongues formed tones, half-tones
from those tons of bronze, icons of sound,
the air thick with their clamorous rounds.

Insufferable God! What could Stalin do
but silence those voices, blow after blow,
beat them like kulaks? Each knell a dead Jew,
White Russian, Pole—he cut the ropes,

tore the belfries down, till, town after town,
straight to the tundra, the ground shuddered
where they crashed, the air gagged
as they were melted, remade into tanks

and guns, those sweet onions peeled down
to nothing, so the sky no longer stung.
What was left went untolled: pen scratch
across parchment, pistol crack blunted

by a bunker door. First the air recoiled,
then thinned, slipped between hinges,
spread in circles, seeking an ear, someone
to hear the body's thud, as one

after another was dragged off
to unmarked dirt, down where silence
blends with copper and tin, where almost
inaudible bones, heaps, half-bones wait

for earth to be unearthed, tongues loosened,
the ringing restored—in town after town,
that cloud-battering bronze, air unbound,
as the bells toll, they tell, each knell.

The Harrowing

Steep concrete stairs leading up to
the empty stadium's ledge—

and was it a moment's lapse,
that one step out onto air?

Or was there a clamor,
a shrieking inside, a pack

chasing her, creatures who prodded
and leered, who for so long,

like sleeping dogs,
she gingerly stepped around,

and perhaps had come to think of
as companions in her widowhood,

as they slumbered and roused,
drove her to the brink, then cowered,

as her grown sons filled her mind,
forcing them back,

until she came to that ledge

where she must have hesitated
in the afternoon light,

the shimmering green of playing fields
and distant hills . . .

☾

Of the three days in the cave,
the Gospels do not speak—nothing
of that journey others have imagined

through inner earth, light-lathed
or dazed with ground fog—
nothing of the harrow teeth,

the hard passage
into the death swamp where souls drift,
some nodding out,

some on angry lookout,
crouched, ready to lunge
and tear at the wounds,

while others leap up eager
to follow, racing ahead,
then running back.

Or would Spirit do this alone,
if indeed it was done—
a heavy wind, a shimmering presence,

while the body lay stiff in its wounds,
lead weight, blood caked,
until—

what?—a rumble of voice,
a prod of light, then the wrenching
ache of flesh—

Impossible to know another's ache,
what brute spirits rush the soul's house,

tumble shelves, trample the lovely books,
ram their heads through picture frames,

toss tables and chairs out the windows,
till blackout's the only relief.

You who would have been Silence to her,
wrecked, solitary as she was,

you who could have been caught
on wings and lifted up, but instead

let yourself be nailed to that dark wood,
believing death a seed, darkness a season,

what of this one, her years past bearing,
who stood on the ledge—

is there a chance that even
in her bitter plunge she might have

seen you in the light, green
and tender, rising toward her?

Prisoner Bonhoeffer

Executed April 9, 1945, Flossenburg Concentration Camp

Better be wordless, he thinks, better Bach's swell
and diminuendo, *cantus firmus*, not quite drowned out

as notes rise and fall, until—is this it?—

the rising and falling are one, God in the midst,
not on some edge beyond, but *in*—

these cold cells, infested blankets, bitter voices.

Thus he writes to friends, "It is not by abstract argument,
but example . . . ," and "leave the insoluble unsolved. . . ."

So little can be spoken in letters,

so much not even hinted, certain hopes, one death
to prevent countless others . . .

Why mention headaches, bad teeth, cramped legs?

Better anthills, bees, the nest of titmice outside his window,
and thank you for the books, and here's a list of others.

And when the *Ethics* goes badly, there's verse—

rhyme to calm desire, temper the nightmares,
bear the new thought: release won't come,

God will not rise up out of war's insane machine

to pull him down from the wooden platform,
halt the order to strip and walk barefoot

up the scaffold steps,

where for him end and beginning are one
with the rope circling his neck

as time drops out from under, and is gone.

An Exchange

After I didn't buy the copper chicken
hung from the shop's tin ceiling, the one
that said Poland to me, and the war just begun,

it kept on talking for days—about gray
clotted skies, wind through barn slats
stirring the soft mumble and flurry of hens.

Snow-patched yards, it said, and a horse
in its coat of frost, swaybacked, staring
as an old woman reaches knotted hands

into hen-warm hay to gather eggs—
the miracle and sad story of eggs,
how whole countries can break,

their hens scurry off, their horses
stumble toward useless barns,
as planes drone through brittle skies.

Hard life, dirt life, rutted tracks, ditches
full of bones and charred foundations
where stables burn, and hens won't lay,

where hens fly off to roost in woods,
to scratch in dirt and peck among lost buttons,
bullet casings, blackened matches.

From her forest perch, what a humble song
a chicken sings, sometimes the last thing
a partisan hears before the coins

are pressed to his eyes, and brethren
quickly strip his boots and gun. Above them,
that little mother of everything fragile,

her fluffed up breast, her snowcapped
cluck and bob—even now she sings,
keeping watch over the ruined world.

Latcho Drom

"Safe Journey"

Nowhere to nest, to rest their heads,
like starlings scattered by gunshot—

a flock of gypsies.
When the town runs them out,

tosses scarves and pots into the street,
then sweeps,

they even roost in an old tree, nail up
ladder rungs, then, limb after limb, add

platforms, cook stoves, cradle slings, hang sheets
for loose billowing walls.

But a town wants roofs, wants rent, rules
to keep the rich rich,

keep the poor shame-faced
behind closed doors—

until the flagrant gypsies come:
until they're chased out, chased up,

until their charred throats, their knife-glint eyes
slide under our buttoned shirts

and find that secret place a song lives,
that choked-back sob tucked inside.

Call it the soul, it slips out
to sit under those windy rooms,

among parrot-bright skirts, raven coats
and the wings of a violin.

All night it lingers in that throb of song,
hearing how the world poisons

fruit-eating birds, shoots a flock
into drifting feathers,

how the road is rough and dark,
but better than the town's spit . . .

At dawn, the town wakes
to wooden wheel clatter, horse hooves,

feel of something missing, snatched.
We don't know what.

Of the Many

My failed fish poem—its cabana-clothed creatures
        in bold stripes and yellow bull's-eyes
        like a retirement town's zoot-suited underground,

My failed lament for the woman dumping her trash
        off the side of the road, finding in the rain-slick ravine
        my friend's body, half his face blown off,

That inadequate elegy for my aunt, whose head ticked
        like a frightened clock, for the blank green eyeballs
        she swallowed at every meal, to see or not see,

My failed dog poem, prison poem, mass grave
        and sparrow poem—

Those little prayers with no wings, no blood—

        Those electric blue bodies with yellow lips and fins,
            those red prison stripes freely swimming in and out,

        That woman seeing my friend's one shocked eye stare up
            among egg shells and bacon rinds like the land itself
            having waited all night for her black bags
            to hit the ground and burst into a shriek,

        My aunt's red bracelets, sandpaper laugh, gin-soaked pity—

Draft after draft, the words pile up, press down,
        till what's beyond words gets crushed—

My lost dog, the inmate asking to learn cursive, "the curly stuff,"
        fields seeded with bones, how many sparrows—

If there's a place where nothing is wasted,
        let them exist there—each fallen bird, each glaring skull
        and chained body

        somewhere found and counted, and sung.

Sacred Heart

Gray skies, fog seeping up from the harbor
through the rougher streets of our town—
it's always winter when I think of him,

how on icy walks he'd scurry
past the saint-crammed Catholic gift shop,
a small skittish man glancing furtively.

Bored punks turned as he passed, then, *forget it*,
they'd lean back, *not worth the hassle* . . .
And so he'd escape unscathed,

our neighborhood pilgrim, cross-wired
and benign, part of SSI's ragged intelligentsia,
exhausted by his meds, but happy

to pin up flyers for galleries and open mikes.
And he was pleased to hover hen-like
over his briefcase of smudged verses

typed off the paper's edge, apocalypse in cross-outs
and coffee rings, where angels fling down fire,
and the poor shake off coats of lead.

I thought what he wanted me to see
in the darkened church were apostles in blue
and red glass robes, their scrawny fingers stretched

toward heaven. But, no, he loved the small
expressionless moon-white faces set in each corner
like children peering in from the cold.

Blank souls, he said, waiting for birth into
our school of sorrows, wanting our bright clothes,
no matter where those colors come from.

Just to sit with them, he'd set out in winter dusk
through a warren of streets and half-streets
as mist thickened its glaze. Some mornings

the janitor would find him curled in a pew,
prayer book open to the place where you could
fill in the names of everything unwanted,

unfinished, given undignified ends.
And now for years to come, whoever turns
the pages of that book, searching for a sign,

will find his jittery ink, and not knowing
of the stones the kids sometimes threw,
or the bus that backed up and killed him,

they'll just see these half-drawn waifs
staring back from the margins, as if in love
with every fumble and ache of flesh.

And over them—I dog-eared the page—
his bright scrawl, *Don't be afraid, Do not*
underscored three times.

Double Portrait

After a photograph by Luis Poirot of Neruda with figurehead

Behind him, she leans out from the wall—
her new prow—with a gaze that even on land
looks glassy, lost in some inner sea.

By his pose he declares himself
son of her glazed eyes and broken beauty,
offspring of that sea-cracked and refurbished face,

as if he too could look through water's endless hues
into its ruins of salt, the sleeping flames
within those tides that grief swells.

His brows, like hers, are raised, but thicker.
The flesh at his throat sags, while she remains
creaseless and mild, with the sad astonishment

of a mother who has seen too far past
the late-night cradle into some harder rocking
of her child's life. The camera's nothing to her,

who was made to sail through time, while he knows
the power of film, and allows himself
to be swirled through darkness and red light,

so he might live in two dimensions
when the third is gone, pressed into words
that depth-charge the soul and raise from its sea floor

cargoes of mangled bells, granite roses,
blue cruets rancid with the dregs of stars,
and all those storm-tossed women and men he loved,

those bright songbirds blown off course by rough winds,
their yellow flames a long way from revolution,
but fueling it just the same.

U.S. Clamps Down on
Pianos to Cuba

All over Cuba, tuneful Cuba, ruin plays
itself out in the backfires of big-finned cars,
in rain dripping from overhangs, waves battering

sea walls—as if to ask, how long can this
musical fortress last? How long in green
humid Cuba before those soft-wood pianos,

once sent by comrades in Europe,
turn into rundown termite hotels?
Back in the 1950s, polished grands

filled every Havana ballroom—
gamblers and glitz, movie stars, mafia dons,
martinis, big bands. Where could all that go,

but under?—those bright bandstands crashing
like Bud Powell in Bellevue, who drew
a keyboard on the hospital wall and played

for visitors, asking how they liked the tune,
his ears so fine he could make music
out of plaster, ghost notes passing through

wall and ear bone. But what happens
to an ear when the soundboard warps,
when the ghost notes drag rusted chains?

To get donated Steinways and Baldwins
into Havana requires cranes, a cargo ship,
then derricks and container trucks,

which aren't on the dock when the ship arrives.
So the young American who's risking
arrest to break this sound barrier

worries and phones, paces and waits.
You'd think pianos were state secrets,
the way he's been tailed by the Feds,

taken in for questioning. *They* couldn't care less
if a prodigy loses her ear, if her fingers fly
at Bach speed straight into a stuck note's thunk.

Word comes down like a fist: No pianos to Cuba.
You'd think our skies never fatten on winds
that first clatter in palm leaves, whistling

through Havana's shutters and wrought iron rails,
that the beat of rain drumming tin buckets
and car roofs can't pass through walls, syncopate

the street, as under overhangs, citizens
gather with trumpets and guitars, the music
in Cuba swelling out of sea-pitted brass

and rusted strings, out of potholes, broken
storm drains, music on every corner,
radios still playing when the cars don't run—

is that possible, radios still playing?—
too much music for anyone to block, the air
heavy with it, and the wind picking up.

Second Line

Blindfolded and gagged, tossed in the back
of a car—it's how they gather up young men
and after tire irons and chains, leave some

lying in the road like dirt, rained on all night.
Some are bundled-up, tossed off a bridge
into the river whose muddy swirls warn:

kick, fight, breathe, twist your arms free.
Some do. They rise, spit out the rags
stuffed in their mouths, limp back to town,

and one begins to sing—slow at first—*Lord,
I want to be in that number* . . . Another moans
a low muted tone where words won't go.

And there's a bridge from verse to verse,
where bodies rise out of thicket and ditch,
out of jail cell, ravine and watery grave,

where gone, invisible hands seem to lift
like drum sticks, and soul sax blood brass
begin to flow, a band improvising

resurrection, until the dead
take to the streets, a spirit insurrection,
dripping river muck and frayed rope—

with crow-pecked eyes, burnt flesh, charred bone,
they rise, every flown soul finding its way
back through troubled air to swell the song.

Vanishing Act

Over the phone we're already bodiless,
though remember, Love, sound has a source,

and even a kiss made of mist
can touch a cheek and lodge in the mind.

Even a rose made of nothing but words.

It's not really a choice to be working on this
vanishing act. We hardly achieve form

before it starts going soft, opinions first,
then all those clamoring ambitions.

I can't help fretting about our next porous
existence, which one of us

will go first, last breath disappearing
in a crowd of molecules,

while the other is left alone
with a closet full of empty clothes.

Still, here on earth, it seems nothing
vanishes completely.

Fire leaves ash, a boat its wake wobbling
against the dock, and once we put our fingers

into the grooves where bullets gouged
the columns of the Dublin post office.

Remember the young gypsy girl who sat
on the curb, her breath already reeking

as she held out that squalling baby
and begged for spare change—

behind her how many curses, evictions,
burning wagons?

Until it's our turn, what do we really know?

Even despair, Kierkegaard said, is good—
enough to make a man

lift out of its withered case a battered violin,
enough to cause a woman

warming herself under five skirts
to throw back her head and sing.

Frayed strings. Scorched throat of song.

First it vanishes into thin air,
then the air enters us.

III

Elegy with Morning Glories

They climb trellis, porch rails, drain spout,
all the way to the roof—a spectacular year,
so passersby stop, and two women argue
over whether or not they're real. Sad thought—

like the time I woke up wondering why
a month has thirty days, until walking home
that night I looked up and saw: Oh, the moon.
How could I forget? Dear City

with your houses packed tight, yellow white white,
your night-black alleys and vacant lots; Unreal
City of shadows, with no moon until
it's high overhead, and then who looks up,

fixed as we are on curbs and sidewalk bricks
upended by roots? Dear City of the stroke
that shook my mother's tree, made her a person
I never met, one who looked at the pool

outside her building and asked what it was—
nineteen years in that place watching her husband
dive, and now it could have been concrete
or the sky he disappeared into and came back out;

City whose crows made her cover her ears
and cry, *stop, stop!*—same voice she used to scold,
only now more shattered, this woman I once
displeased, I, the crow, the crasher, my taste for trash,

always wearing something that raised her brow,
dizzying myself under blurry stars, coming home late,
and talking, talking, which was against the rules
in our house where so much was kept unspoken—

I never thought she'd grow so fragile, so lost
looking out the window, she'd ask if that streetlight
was the moon. If so, think how many we'd have
lining the roads, each one disposable, replaceable.

She who was my start, my star, has burned out,
and though her light still flickers in the blue
dusk she loved, the blue flowers that unswirl
each morning, though I think I see her

in a white sun hat arguing they must be real
or they couldn't climb so high, she is gone,
and nowhere beside any trellis, or any doorsill
in this city, will there ever be another.

Belmullet

To see where I came from, I'm looking at stones,
at *Johns* and *Marys*, at twenty-eight *Nearys*
in a County Mayo graveyard, each with a pot
of primroses, a plot with white chips of gravel.

If the Irish love talk, my family's silence
seemed to ask, Who wants to go back
to rotten potatoes and patched-up boats,
horse thievery and peat? Who needs long roots

and old wars? Those sealed lips clearly said,
Better to shrug it all off, scrape the sod
from your boots and glad-hand the new world,
let mild winds drift above gravity's grip.

But what wind doesn't come from elsewhere?
Now that those Nearys are nearly gone,
and there's no one to ask whose history
is swelling my knuckles, crimping my face,

I want to be part of a line tethered somewhere,
if only by sea swells, by gusts I love best
when they batter. So I stand among stones
cut deep with my name, not knowing

if the bones rusting here in this ground
are related. But since my family left
no word, I tell these Nearys, if they'll have me,
I'd be pleased to be ghosted by them

in their Wellies and wool, their prayer beads
and pints, their eyes creased by sea glitter
and those minor chords with bent notes
piercing the soul. I'd be pleased

to root myself in this town where tides rise
and sink into sludge, this river mouth littered
with bike frames, clumps of mussels,
and plastic paint buckets—my roots in this junk

the water will nudge and cover again,
as it pours through the inlet, swirling with foam.
Is this where I come from? I kneel down
to finger the gouged letters and half-think,

half-say to this long line of Marys and Johns,
these twenty-eight Nearys: If we all come
to the same end, surely it's not just malarkey
and lark song spiraling up, then plummeting

silently down, surely by sun glint and gull,
by that long ago swallowed sadness,
by sea gut and gravel and wind-wild sky,
these stones that name you name me as well.

Famine

No one's left who watched the crop
go to rot, till even its eye roots oozed.

And the stench—like something the ground
spat out, then worse, the fields caught,

infected right to the doorstep,
knobby lumps gone to mush in the hand.

No one's left of all those who trudged
toward the sea, stomachs so hollow

every inedible rock along the road
must have looked like a bitter potato

they'd gladly break their teeth on.

Now at the market varieties are heaped
in bin after bin, dirt-spackled bulbs,

aortas of earth—some from Peru
called *papa*, so I think of my father's heart

that gave out before I knew him, arteries
clogged in early blight. Sometimes

making dinner, I lift a potato
to my ear as if even the drub

of absolute silence could be a root.
Later I drink the cooled cooking broth

as I've been taught, so nothing is lost.

Waiting Room

Don't ask me about my father—
if he sang to me, if I ever dissolved on his chest like a pill
on a tongue, if his brows were as black as I remember,
his grin as horsey.

I can name four rivers, the president, I know what day it is,
but don't ask me if art can save anyone.

And don't ask me about my father.

On a scale from 1 to 10, I am an unknown quantity,
anything I say may be against me.

Snowflakes like people never think anything is their fault.

Where my father is
everyone has stone eyes, penny eyes, bone hollows
where water pools. The only sound is rain seeping
like a dog endlessly licking itself.

My education
was a corset with bone stays and strings yanked tight,
something worn now only in brothels, to tease.

I am here because last night my mind split between euphoria
and grief. Someone was dying, someone was embracing,
and I couldn't make the stove turn on. I held a match
and had too many ideas for how to use it.

The dead live in a country where nobody talks.
In dreams, just as I am about to enter, I wake up
frantic to unstick my mouth.

I am here because every moment's a casket I am trying to flee
before the lid drops.

Wood Shedding

This close to the instrument you can hear breath entering the sax's brass, and the clack of keys, sound going out to the wall which sends it back, breath's invisible bubbles lingering briefly before they break, high notes like leaves wind-snatched from a bough, like glitter on a sunlit bay, so much inside the soul, and who knew it could be this fluid, who knew the air had streams, could split its seams, rise twig-high then drop through pitted brass to root rumble, moss in the mouth, splinter and knot of song, eyes in its unpainted beams, each note a wound, a limb snapped off, broken bough, gone, but the scar sweet, the sap beaded up like an undertone's aftermath, its moth-bump against a light bulb sizzling out—far out, gone, Man: that feeling in the gut, a tune's slide to the lowest keys, to the day's last light honeyed and long, heading into sultry Scotch straight up, window flare and rust light, street lamps flickering down the avenue's blue, slow ride toward midnight, black and white cloud light, star-tossed, red eye of plane flashing over a club's closed door, grill down, but the vibe lingers on cindery streets, steaming grates, the notes slipping through wires and stark trees, along the slats of a broken shutter in the bluest hour of night, hour of God, of train gone, smoker in a doorway, match strike of footsteps on concrete, one hunched walker dog-leashed to a thin leaf-scrap of moon, its high C barely audible over the silent changes of traffic lights in this dark pocket of night, where nothing that drifts is a stranger and everyone awake knows the score.

Shrines

In Donegal we climbed over a cow gate,
crossed through a field among hooded crows
and earth smells, climbed a stile and stepped onto
rain-mucked ground, to enter a small grotto
where a stone Saint Colum was surrounded by

a yellow cigarette lighter, a key ring with green gremlin, a rain-swollen
missal, toy train, crumpled cigarette pack, inhaler, cassette tape, small
heart-shaped stone . . .

and we wondered what the saint made of all this.
Would he read minds anxious over a dying parent,
a mean boyfriend, sullen daughter, the plant closing,
pub going broke? These things don't say,
Blast me with light, Make me rich,
but something more like

> *Will I get through this?*
> *Me and the missus, will we laugh again?*
> *Will the cough go away?*

A shot glass with small dried asters beginning to shed, a Spiderman
with moveable limbs, nail clippers, plastic daisy, three Euros holding
down a pink banknote . . .

《

Back home, in the prison art room, I said,
Everyone toss onto the table something precious,
and we'll make a still life:

a packet of artificial sweetener, ID badge, pen, one cigarette, pair
of glasses, the dog-eared photo of a toothless boy grinning under a
cowboy hat, and *Here*—one joker said, with a card-flinging gesture—*the*
invisible keys to the kingdom,

which probably meant outside, freedom to him,
though I thought of the holding pen between
electric doors where, each week as we waited,
sometimes for ten minutes, he'd play king
of that tiny domain, lining us up to mug
for the guards watching on closed-circuit TV.

❮

A rubber finger, rusted harmonica, empty whiskey bottle, leather
change purse, small wrench, penknife, child's sippy cup . . .

We stood in the rain, our pant legs mud splattered,
gazing at all these things, wondering what they said.

> *There must be a view from the other side*
> *where things look different, and if it please you,*
> *if you'd give me a glimpse . . .*

> *I know I don't come here enough,*
> *but if you'll forgive me my withheld*
> *car keys and wallet, I'll leave you this*

crucifix, this cuff link, tube of lipstick, coin my thigh has warmed,
this bicycle light, this one leather glove, and

> *Here's the Barbie I've been playing with*
> *in the back seat.*

> *Here's my feckin' wedding ring—*
> *take it is all I ask.*

> *Take my exams, take the weight, the sadness,*
> *the crazy thoughts, my parents screaming,*
> *the whiskey stink, the cough.*

> *Please, I just want a little sign.*

❮

Wrist watch, newspaper clipping, pair of smudged glasses, hospital
wristband, necklace with half a heart, a letter broken on its crease
lines . . .

Are these the entry fees for the invisible kingdom, where

> *I've already dropped a dime and my time's not up,*
> *I am so freaking bored I'm in poetry class*
> *with these losers, these bottom dwellers, slime,*
> *my brothers, and the only prayer I've got*
> *is, Just fucking do it, break me—*

a kingdom, which if it can't be seen could be anywhere, even here,
unlocked by something as simple as

a shirt button with its little antenna of thread, a ceramic pin *I made
in art class for my mother, but here, you take it*, this poem *I wrote late last
night in my cell, I'm sorry, it rhymes . . . ,*

and here in this open ball cap I have passed
around the room for each of us to drop in
one word for what we fear most, all of them
come down to being: *rejected*
lonely, abandoned . . .

Is anyone listening?

In Donegal, were the saint's arms extended
like Jesus' or folded in prayer? I can't remember,
I was so stunned to enter that wild heap,
that jumbled array—shattered whiskey bottle,
rusted scissors, chewed pencil, flashlight—
some requests clear,

while the whole grotto insisted on a kingdom,
invisible as it is, an other side
from which these things look different,
maybe not like *things* at all.

At the Window

If the doctor's new machine is right, my eyes
are turning into old window glass, warped,
distorted at a thousand points, watching
the moon's fine edge start to fray. But it's spring,

and as if our rooms perched in its branches,
a flowering tree fills the windows. How easy
to say *as if*—as if we were that couple of tiny
Northern Parulas, flitting from limb to limb,

as if we had flown all night, then dropped down
through power lines to feed at first light,
exhausted and starving, intent on the journey,
impelled to breed, breed, always more life.

My grandmother of the Coke-bottle lenses,
of the enormous blue eyes flying close
to the glass like a creature about to crash,
used to recite when she stumbled, "'I see,'

said the blind man when he bumped into the light,"
which I only recalled after slamming into
the plate glass I must have thought was a door—
or didn't think at all, lost inside my head,

as I charged full speed into spectacle-snap,
black-eye smack, at which I saw suddenly
how much I didn't see at all, with a whole
restaurant watching. When a bird flies

into glass does it pass from stun to sob,
and have to make up a new song, or does it
shake off the shock and go on where it was headed
all along, forget reflection? "I once . . . was blind,

but now I see," John Newton wrote, and then
gave up his slave ship to grieve all the ruin
he had wrought. But *how* did he come to see—
what shock, what light shattered the old lens?

Until I really looked, I thought geese flew
in those perfect V's we were taught in school,
which would make this flock heading north not
geese at all, with their constantly changing stream

of unraveling threads, their one straggler
wildly flapping to catch up, that outsider
squawking a different tune. Now a small breeze
flies into the tree, so its blossoms flutter,

and a few tear loose to rise, to drift briefly
in the otherwise unseeable air,
that invisible substance we call nothing
and can't live two minutes without.

Bass Flute

No talk here of *Meaning*, it's all *-ing*,
raw urge that nudges the wall between
music and noise. Now the man kisses

his mouthpiece, hums it into a swarm
buzzing out from the silver hive. Now
it's the sound of key clatter and wheeze,

sound of the unmuffled gut set free
to bluster and honk, the drowsy heart
ungagged, as if this instrument wants

to be more than notes on a page: demands
to be amped up past soothing ooohs, oomphed out
through spheres, ousted far beyond *fa-la-la*.

It pulls the man to his toes, then bends him
in half. It wants to be bad, to beatbox,
batter his breath, hiss and clang like steam heat.

It wants to riff till the rafters fall, and won't
let the man go until it's emptied him out,
soul and sweat and spit.

Cedar Waxwings

I did not think one was your father, come back
quick-eyed, eager to debate again,

or my sister's frail husband
in his red-striped apron, unbandaged and ravenous.

I just wanted to watch those little bolts of life
flitting from limb to limb, so many

some had to hang upside down
to pluck and slurp the wizened berries.

With their yellow tail fringe they swooped in,
the whole tawny flock, that box of matches,

red tipped—ready to strike, to unhinge, unhelm,
overwhelm the jagged March trees.

I did not imagine our nephew
in his yellow sweater, no longer wheezing,

or your brother under stage lights,
tenor sax at his lips, filling it with breath, riffing

notes like flocked birds flashing down from higher trees,
to gobble more and more fermented berries,

till they teeter off their limb and have to flap
themselves back.

All those faces we'll never see again
look up, suddenly quickened and bright—

despite so many gone, or *because*,
we listen to that shrill, that shush and chuck

in the hawthorns across the street,
which I do not imagine into words.

After all, what would they say, so far gone
into their cups, lifting glass after glass?

Well, let them.
Let them guzzle and swill, chatter and flap

till it's all berry mash, rusted hinge, mud helm, mayhem,
and what's left of us here on the ground, undone.

Meenala, County Donegal

We slept in the house like birds
    nestled on a ship's mast, waves
        of wind rocking us, buffeting
back and forth, as the windows
    throbbed and drinking glasses
        teetered toward toppling—
or did I dream that, nested
    as I was in the bed's deep
        billow, and *not* driving, not
white-knuckled on narrow lanes,
    hard packed ruts where sheep settled
        in sleep, where fuchsia hedges
loomed in headlights—no little
    hothouse plants from home hung in
        baskets, but huge shrubs hiding
the road's drop, so to veer off
    would burst a rain of blossoms
        onto the rental car's ruin.
Adrift in bed, loose, listing
    toward sleep, I saw those woolly
        ewes holding the road in place,
then swarmed by wind, swirling up
    into clouds—everything *up*
        in bright fluff, blossomy gusts.
We woke in the downy roost
    our friends had made for us, sleep-
        tumbled by that air ocean's
bluster and roar. So this is
    a gale, we said. But, No, no,
        nothing near that force, they grinned.
We wondered then what they knew
    of a breath that could batter
        doors to unhinging, hammer
and bang at windows, wanting in—
    some kind of wild spirit-shove
        turning the world inside out.

Traps and Groove

I couldn't begin to tap it out,
not even then, on the hood of my car,
last Saturday night—no, Friday,

after I had driven across the river
to the restaurant where friends were waiting,
after I parked so well just one door down,

in front of some club's spray-painted wall
with words like birds grown fat over skulls
and leaves, words with sharp beaks, spread wings,

in front of which young men were bunched,
their thoughts turning to smoke, little clouds
of chuckle and grunt, past which my cautious half,

with fixed-bayonet eyes, wanted to charge
straight into fine dining. But not so quick,
I thought. Somewhere behind that wall,

there's a high-hat, a snare, a couple of toms,
and a drummer getting loved all over by God.
I could hear the sticks' scatter and stitch,

brushes sweeping what must be the moon's skin,
then cymbals and a clatter of bright shards,
everything in drum light, our breath, our blood.

My square, 4/4 self, wanting her chair
at the table, and a waiter to take orders—
what does she know about backbeat and swing?

Despite her, my hips picked up something
the drums were saying from inside that club,
something I could almost, any minute, join—

a door about to blow open, right there,
where it's been made out of spray paint on brick
by somebody called FURZ, whose name looks

like a red bird just emerging or about
to get lost in a tangle of thick foliage,
hard to say which.

Out of Nowhere

Slow drum brush, the Hammond B-3
    comping a solo sax, and nothing
        on your mind but the ice in your glass
shifting like notes played one at a time,
    like minutes melting in the dark drift
        of everything past, old goals, scores
wiped clean as the barkeep's tumblers.
    Nobody wants to scratch, to scorch, to fold.
        Yet tonight you think what else is there,
as you flash on the schoolroom sign
    from years ago, telling you "Zero
        is the number of things you have
when you have nothing." Nothing tonight
    but the sax handing off the lead
        to the organ's bluesy prayer,
as you close your eyes, and slow dance
    yourself, empty-handed, letting
        your one heart do nothing but go on.
What else is there? Night turns blue
    and an old fear fills your mind—
        one wrong move, all you could lose.
Another round, and it's all round,
    washed in an amber swirl, where you
        know things you can never say,
though they keep you awake, safe
    from the bluff of pride, that bright lie
        you crashed from years ago
and don't want back. Whatever you lack
    you'll take this ballad's slow drag,
        its low-down mellow sound,
the Hammond's soulful plea pitched
    to the heart's bittersweet beat
        hitting the bottom of this tune,

as the sax stretches out its closing bars,
wanting nothing more than to linger
here, where a voice—it could be yours—
rises out of midnight's throat, to give
this song and everything it knows
a lone and barely whispered, *Yes.*

Election Day

Falling on the steps of city hall, the light
this late afternoon infuses the whole sky
and bathes these poor little trees of heaven
stuck in concrete. From all sides, flooding down,

light slants across ruddy brick storefronts,
streaks along cables, glitters up from the bay,
and now, as I turn west toward the hospital,
here's the moon, the Cheshire moon, grinning

bright as a politician's promise, only better,
not favoring a few, but shining for anyone
who stops to gaze at this sky, which not even
the coldest facts can make less marvelous

just now, before the tabulations begin.
And here's the hospital, grinding on, full
of wires and tubes, trays of food, socks that
puff up and down so my friend's legs don't clot.

Isn't it wonderful?—her loopy rainbow grin,
her dozing off mid-sentence, waking surprised,
to say, "Oh, hello," as if I just arrived.
And now when I say good-bye and step out,

the sky's so deep I want to stuff the ballot box,
voting for earth all over again, happy to shiver
in the glow, as the first stars poke through
this impossible to name, not-yet-midnight blue,

letting it pour over me—glorious night,
the brightening moon, below which we turn
in endless space, all of us afloat, held
by invisible strings, though we feel so solid,

so full of our own weight. Lord, let me stand here
feeling nothing but this moment, spinning
and not dizzy, not yet facing the election results.
Let the bass from this passing car pulse through me

as the tattered man leaning on the streetlight
stops another, just to ask the name of his dog,
nothing more, just to say that name, *Herbie*,
and knuckle his ears. Amazing: Two men,

one in a fine suit, one in frayed tweed, stop
and chat, shake hands, each grinning as they part—
here, under this glowing sky, the polls still open,
and the moon above, new, all over again.

To a Plum

Love child of summer,
born of a bird cry and the blue moon,

no wonder you can't make up your mind
between magenta and mist, honey

and blood. Between night
and the sun-struck bay, you hang

heavy on the limb, your blue-black
powdery sheen like shimmering kimono silk

the color of midnight and bruise.
What's there to lose?

What glass, wine wobbling at the rim,
doesn't long to spill,

what sweet fruit wouldn't split
its skin to release the juicy light

hidden within? Ah, but once it's out,
there's no stuffing it back.

And that hint of frost glazing your flesh,
its hue the dark of winter mulch?

Clearly there's no praising you
without praising the sugary rune

you come to, wrinkled lips licked
by the moon's dark.

Pears, Unstolen

I was stopped on the sidewalk by pears
glowing on their tree like antique ornaments
with flaking paint, a green metallic shimmer
hinting at yellow, mottled with a few flecks of red.

As light flickered over them, they seemed
to flutter like candles in the leaves.
But no—they were pears, and probably hard,
I told myself, probably inedible, and holding

their juices tight, if they had juices at all.
Besides, something was pitting them like brass,
splotching, as if trying to spoil. Still, I wanted them.
I wanted that September light licking each fruit,

so it seemed lit from without and within,
a fleshy tallow. I wanted the season's clock
stopped before the next strike, stopped in this
amber afternoon, my walk halfway,

the shiny leaves just starting to curl,
but still far from falling, and the pears
half hidden among them like birds singing
so sweetly you step closer, peer in,

careful, careful, wanting to touch that song,
but not squelch it. I stood there wanting
to hoard time, a thief wanting to steal
a song I couldn't hear, a fool believing

there's something sweet that won't disappoint,
that pears in the hand could be anything
like pears dreamed in the mind, or one moment
stopped could keep the rest from rotting.

But what's so bad, a thief will ask: How is
plucking a piece of fruit worse than worms
tunneling in, bees sating themselves
on that honeyed light, or mold blotching it?

Maybe a saint has an answer to that,
something about how too much sweetness spoils,
or how another sweetness grows within.
For weeks I went back and forth, stopping

at the tree, watching first one pear let go
of its limb, then others begin to fall,
flickering briefly like coals in the grass,
before they shrivel, letting their seeds slip out.

"That's the way it goes," mutters the thief.
"As scripture says they must," muses the saint,
while a few last pears glow on their brittle stems
and the wind-strummed boughs bend toward earth.

The Aging Singer

Her mouth is cut with crevices
like a marionette's. That little pout,
so flirty in youth, has turned to a scowl.
Still, the voice—it's all sugar and satin, grit,
tough mama strut, then down-on-the-knee
bluesy plea. She can make one word go on
and on—*Oh Lord, puh-leeeze*—rising higher
till we teeter on a ladder top—*send me—*

while the drum nail-guns, the guitar climbs its frets
adding rung after rung, as if to reach heaven
on sound alone. But—*Lord, Lord—*
she's been around, seen how it topples,
so drops to the gutter of her range,
the strain where gospel shifts from style
to soul wrestling its angel, worn and wounded,
but not letting go. *Lord, please send me—*

and in this small venue she must feel us
listening, our separate thoughts silenced,
as she pours herself out, this diva backed
by young men half amused, half awed, a little
bored, and silenced now, by her raised arm,
as she steps out beyond their licks,
hand beating time on her rippling thigh.
Gone, whatever we thought it took

to make a show, just this voice now, all rust
and cut glass—*send me*—gouging her face,
raking that throat, hardly a voice at all, nothing
left but the lowest note she can score—
someone to—she barely mouths the phrase,
head bowed, mike dropped to her side, and us
on the edge of our seats, as the last
unspoken word fills our minds.

NOTES

"Tidal" is for my sister, Martha Folts.

"Rahsaan": The epigraph and some material in the poem come from *Bright Moments: The Life and Legacy of Rahsaan Roland Kirk*, by John Kruth (Welcome Rain Publishers).

"Bird Lives" is for Paul Lichter.

"What's Left of Heaven": The epigraph comes from *My Life*, by Marc Chagall (Da Capo Press).

"Goldfinch": The epigraph and quoted lines come from *The Selected Poems of Osip Mandelstam*, translated by Clarence Brown and W. S. Merwin (New York Review of Books).

"Russian Bells": The poem was inspired by reading "The Bells: How Harvard Helped Preserve a Russian Legacy," by Elif Batuman, in the April 27, 2009, issue of *The New Yorker*.

"The Harrowing" is in memory of Deborah Digges.

"Prisoner Bonhoeffer": The poem draws on a reading of *Letters and Papers from Prison*, by Dietrich Bonhoeffer, edited by Eberhard Bethge (Macmillan Company).

"*Latcho Drom*": The poem is inspired by a scene in the film of the same title by Tony Gatlif.

"Sacred Heart" is in memory of Fred Schwartz.

"Double Portrait": The photograph by Luis Poirot is on the cover of *Neruda: Selected Poems*, edited by Nathaniel Tarn (Houghton Mifflin Company).

"U.S. Clamps Down on Pianos to Cuba": The poem draws on the documentary about Benjamin Treuhaft's efforts to supply Cuba with pianos, *Tuning with the Enemy* (Ovation).

"Vanishing Act" is for Doug Sholl.

"Wood Shedding" is in memory of David Sholl.

"Bass Flute" is for Carl Dimow.

"Meenala, County Donegal" is for Annie and Ted Deppe.

"The Aging Singer": The six words come from a Percy Mayfield song, "Please Send Me Someone to Love."